A FIELD GUIDE TO
Succulents

Colors, Shapes and Characteristics
For Over 200 Amazing Varieties

MISA MATSUYAMA

TUTTLE Publishing

Tokyo | Rutland, Vermont | Singapore

CONTENTS

Why I Wrote This Book

This book was created with the idea of sharing how attractive succulents are and how fun they are to grow. With that in mind, we've included close-up photos like you've never seen before. Regardless of whether a plant is a small or large type, I wanted to create an atmosphere where you can see the details with a magnifying glass. It would be great if succulents fans could have the chance to really see these finer points, almost as if from the perspective of a succulent. Succulents are full of mysterious charm. They both surprise and delight, and they'll never bore you. Their energy is truly amazing!

—Misa Matsuyama
sol x sol

Growing Succulents Well

Growing succulents is very easy compared to other plants, as they are resistant to both heat and cold. But of course they are living creatures, so while they may not need a lot of watering, they do need to be cared for. It's important to understand your plants' characteristics, so read the basic information carefully in order to understand and meet your succulents' needs.

Tools and Materials for Growing Succulents

Growing succulents is very easy. The tools shown below are the only ones you'll need. The soil should be breathable and water-retentive.

(1) **Fertilizer** Add a small amount as base fertilizer when planting.

(2) **Peat moss** Used as soil when planting in a small container. Not optimal for large containers.

(3) **Akadama soil (medium grain)** Used as pot bottom soil due to its breathability and drainage when planting in large pots.

(4) **Pumice** A natural soil conditioner used as both potting soil and decorative stone.

(5) **Spoon** Convenient for filling small spaces with soil. Used for detailed work.

(6) **Tweezers** This tool is a must! Used for handling cacti, removing dead leaves, and planting.

(7) **Soil scoop** A tool for filling pots and gaps with soil. They come in various sizes, so use according to the size of the plant and container.

(8) **Newspaper** When planting indoors, place it underneath for a simple workspace. Can also be used as a substitute for or in combination with a pot bottom net.

(9) **Soil for succulents** Soil blend that's specifically for succulents. Sand and charcoal are mixed with small granules of Akadama clay as a base.

(10) **Watering can** A pot like this or a container with a single mouth or spout will do the job. Makes watering more fun.

(11) **Scissors** Used for cutting seedlings and roots. Those with good blades are less likely to destroy the plants.

(12) **Brush** Cleans the work area and removes dirt from pots and leaves. Easy-to-use small size.

(13) **Dish cloth** Wrapped around a cactus to prevent the thorns from pricking your hands, so you can use it as a glove.

Watering Succulents

Succulents grow naturally in very dry areas, so they are quite drought-tolerant and will hold up well even if you skip a little watering. On the other hand, overwatering can damage plants. The trick is to strike a balance in the watering cycle. Depending on the season and variety, some plants require very little water for as long as a month. Frequent watering for a succulent can amount to just once every ten days or so. So let's get familiar with watering succulents.

Seasonal watering

The season in which succulent plants grow and store water corresponds with the rainy months of the plant's place of origin. Just like sunlight, the watering method will depend on whether the plant's growing season is summer or winter. To ascertain the growing season, refer to the information that comes with your plant. For the plants in this book, a key to the growing, blooming, dormant, and peak viewing seasons is provided for each genus.

SUMMER TYPES

A variety that grows between spring to fall. From around April when the weather gets warmer, water the plants generously. During the rainy months, keep it moist only when the sun is shining. In the middle of summer, if you water it during the day, the water may become too warm, so it is best to water in the evening or nighttime. In winter, the plant becomes less active and enters a dormant period, so watering about once a month is fine. Many succulents are summer type.

WINTER TYPES

One of the characteristics of the winter type is that it doesn't like the heat very much. Gradually reduce watering during the rainy months and move to a semi-shaded, well-ventilated area. In the summer, the plant enters the dormancy period, so please water it about once a month in the evening or at night. From around October, gradually resume watering. However, it is best to water sparingly during the extremely cold season, as growth slows down.

DORMANT IN WINTER

Summer-type succulents go dormant in winter (December to February). During this period, look for days that are warmer than others and water about ⅓ of the usual amount in the morning. Winter-type succulents go dormant in the summer (April to August). During this period, look for the cooler days and water about ⅓ of the usual amount at night.

How to water a plant without a hold at the bottom of the pot

Pots without holes in the bottom (beakers, cups, etc.) require extra work. After watering until the soil is moist enough, tilt the pot to remove excess water from the bottom. This will help prevent root rot. Leaving standing water can cause root rot and ultimately kill the plant.

Where to Place Succulents

Succulents thrive in dry, sunny areas. Even if you grow a succulent indoors, it will grow quickly if you raise it in an environment that's close to its natural one. A sunny, well-ventilated location is ideal. Succulents do not like dark, humid/damp places, so it is best to keep them in a well-lit place for at least four hours a day.

When managing outdoors

Place plants under an awning, overhang or similar, which provides shade and protects plants from direct exposure to rain. It is best to bring your plants indoors during the rainy months. Avoid placing your plant too deeply in the shade, as it will need some sunlight. It's best to move the pot according to the movement of the sun. Be careful of placing plants directly on concrete or asphalt in the summer. The surface may become too hot due to the reflection of the sun, which will cause burn.

When managing indoors

Indoor spaces don't get as much sunlight as outdoor ones, so choose a place with plenty of sunlight, such as by the window. Succulents don't like humidity very much, so it's a good idea to open the window occasionally to air out the space. Even if the light is bright enough to the human eye, it is often not sufficient for succulents. If your plant seems a bit low-energy, take it outside frequently and let it bask in the sun. If you pay attention to the sun and ventilation, you can easily manage succulents indoors. Also some varieties are resistant to humidity, so they can adorn spaces like kitchens and bathrooms.

Seasonal Care

The bodies of succulents are mostly made up of water, and are designed to store water, so they require little watering. Another characteristic of succulents is that they love light. In the absence of light, the leaves become flimsy, like bean sprouts, and start losing color. In this section, we will introduce basics such as watering and placement according to the season.

SPRING

Spring is known as the growing season for most living things; this also applies to more than half of known succulents. The higher the temperature, the more active the roots, and the faster the soil in the pot will dry out. This means the plant will need watering. If the surface is dry, give it plenty of water. Spring is also the time to take out the plants that were kept indoors during winter so they can breathe natural air and feel the sun. But be careful! The sun is strong, and a lot of sudden exposure may cause burn. Choose a cloudy day to put your plant outside, or drape it with a bit of newspaper until it gets used to outdoor light. On cold, frosty days, bring your plants indoors at night.

SUMMER

Summer is a tough season for succulents. At this time of year, the humidity is high in many regions. The water in the air alone is enough for the plants to survive, so avoid watering during this period. Only small varieties will wilt and wither if they are not watered for about three months, so check the condition of the leaves and water them on a cool night. Avoid direct sunlight and keep in shade. When managing indoors, pay attention to ventilation. Avoid placing plants in a closed room as much as possible. A room with an air conditioner or fan is fine, but avoid allowing air to blow on the plants directly.

FALL

It's the season to rejuvenate succulents that have been damaged and weakened during the summer. Once it gets cooler and the leaves start to turn red (page 12), please resume watering. The plants' now-skinny bodies need to take in water to become plump and healthy and grow again. Move plants that have been resting in the shade during summer to a brighter location. If you place them where the sun is weak, they will not turn red. If you keep them in a sunny place and expose them to enough sunlight, you can enjoy the fall leaves with beautiful colors.

WINTER

Succulents have an image of being vulnerable to the cold, but that's actually not the case, and they can easily survive the winter. As the temperature drops, reduce the frequency of watering to prevent frost damage. If you reduce the water, the concentration in the plant will become thicker and will not freeze. Just as during summer, water sparingly, then stop watering completely, especially for varieties that are vulnerable to cold. Varieties that are weak to the cold will drop their leaves and go completely dormant. Such varieties should be kept indoors; hold off watering until spring, and wait until the plant begins to sprout. Place it on the windowsill during the day and expose it to sunlight. At night, the window will be cold, so move the plant to a warmer spot.

How to Propagate Succulents

One of the charming aspects of succulents is that they are very easy to propagate. Here, we introduce the orthodox methods of propagating succulents: leaf cutting, beheading, and root dividing. It is also important to keep the plants looking good by cutting them back and replanting them. The best time to do this is during the growing season in spring or fall.

Leaf Cutting

This very simple way to propagate involves carefully removing the leaves from the base of the plant and placing them on top of the soil. You don't need to plant the leaf into the soil. When removing the leaves, make sure to pluck them off carefully from the base, or else they may not have a growth point and may not sprout. This method takes a little longer than other methods, but it is easy and can be done with leaves that have come off during repotting and watering. Most succulents can be propagated this way, but it is not suitable for large varieties of Cotyledon, Senecio, and Echeveria.

<table>
<tr><td>Items you'll need</td></tr>
<tr><td>• succulent (or leaves that have dropped off)
• dry soil
• pan</td></tr>
</table>

1 Prepare succulent leaves. If you are using a leaf that dropped off on its own, then it's fine as it is. If you plan to use a leaf from a healthy succulent, let the plant dry out a little before removing a leaf, rather than immediately after watering.

TIP

Since new spouts emerge from the bases of the leaves, if the bases of the leaves are not clean, the plant will not grow well. To remove the leaf try wiggling it side to side carefully.

2 Spread the dry soil in the pan and even it out.

3 Lay out the leaves one by one. The leaves should be placed on their backs, not on their sides. Do not put the tips of the leaves into the soil; simply place them on top.

4 After you've arranged all the leaves, wait for the roots and spout to emerge. During this time, refrain from watering. Water may enter through the leaf tips and cause rotting. Also, too much light will dry them out, so keep them indoors and away from direct sunlight.

5 After a few days, when the roots emerge from the leaves, you can start watering. At this step, if the roots are sticking out of the soil, make a shallow hole in the soil with tweezers and lightly pour soil over the roots to bury them.

6 After a few days, new sprouts should emerge. When the leaves finish nourishing the sprout, they will gradually wither and become completely crumbly. Until this happens, grow the plants with the leaf attached, and remove the leaf when it has completely withered.

Growth Process of leaf cutting

Day 14
Roots are growing little by little.

Day 29
Roots emerge and the sprout grows bigger.

Day 72
Size varies individually, but they are growing.

Day 120
Growing even bigger. After this, when the leaf dies, plant them in a container of your choice.

Beheading

This is a common method of propagating by cutting off the head and planting the cutting into soil. Succulents can also be easily grown in this way. It's best to dry them in the shade for 4–5 days before planting them. Sedums and Aeoniums will take about 10 days, Crassula about 15–20 days, and Senecio, Cotyledon, and Echeveria about 20 days to 1 month to grow roots. This propagating method can be used with stem cuttings from overgrown branches.

Preparation

- overgrown succulent (we're using a toliman stonecrop)
- dried soil

1

Hold the head of the succulent and cut the stem from a little below the base of it.

2

After cutting, you will see only the stem and it will look lonely, but if you leave it alone...

...after a few days, a new sprout will emerge from the sides of the parent plant.

3

Remove about 2–3 lower leaves off the cutting. If we were to leave it as it is, soil may cover the leaves, causing them and, eventually, the entire cutting to rot.

4

Dry the cut end of the cutting. At this step, refrain from watering. If the cutting is laid down to dry, it might start to bend, making it difficult to plant later. So instead, place the cutting in a container where you can have it dry straight up (as shown in the photo). Keep the cutting in a well-ventilated, shady area.

The cutting shown at right is bent because it was dried in a recumbent position.

5

After a few days, the roots develop as shown in the photo.

6

Once the cuttings have rooted, plant them in a container of your choice to complete the process.

Root Division

This method involves digging up a large plant and dividing the roots to create a new plant. The best time to do this is when replanting or when there are too many plants growing in clusters. This method is best suited for succulents such as Aloe and Haworthia, which have separate offspring growing from the base of the plant. Remove the plant from the pot along with the entire potting medium, take and plant the offspring. Unlike a shoot, the root system is already present in the plant, so once the plant is divided, plant it immediately without allowing it to dry out, water it, then water again after 5–10 days.

Preparation

- fully grown succulent
- newspaper
- scoop
- akadama soil
- fertilizer
- tweezers
- soil
- pot

1

Prepare the succulent you want to divide. Tap the pot lightly, insert tweezers into the edge, and depot the plant by lifting it from the bottom.

2

The state of the roots after the plant is depotted.

3

Remove old soil from the roots by hand. If the roots are too tangled, it is good to tidy then up a little.

4

Tidied up roots.

5

This time we'll be dividing the plant into 3 pieces. (In the case of this plant, you can divide it into 4, but if the offspring are too small, they may not survive.)

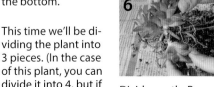

6

Divide gently. Be careful not to separate the child plant from its roots, if there are any.

7

Divided plant. If the separated plant is big, dry it for a day or so before replanting.

8

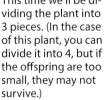

Finish planting in each container. For the planting method, refer to Repotting on page 10.

Cutting and Replanting

As a succulent grows, it often becomes unbalanced. A simple way to care for it is to cut it, then replant the cutting into the same pot. Just as with root dividing (page 9), you can depot it with a pair of tweezers. It's best to do this when the roots are dry so make sure to wait about a week after watering to cut and replant.

1 Overgrown succulent.

2 Leaving about 3 lower leaves, cut the leaves closest to the base.

3 If the cutting is long, it's fine to trim it as long as you leave enough stem for replanting.

4 Remove the lower leaves so that they can be easily planted into soil.

5 Leaves removed. Clearing away the lower leaves allows more air to circulate around the base of the cutting, preventing rot.

6 Prepare your other cuttings in the same way.

7 Hold the stem with tweezers and plant it into the soil.

8 Check the balance of the plants and place them in the soil as desired.

9 Finished. Hold off on watering for about 10 days. If the seedling is firm to the touch, you'll know that rooting is established. Once the cuttings have rooted, you can resume usual care.

Repotting

After growing in the same pot for a few years, the plant may appear to be a little cramped due to the formation of new plantlets. Also, the roots in the pot can catch disease, so in such cases, repot the plant to a larger pot. Avoid doing this in mid-summer and mid-winter. The best time to do this is in the cooler months during spring and fall.

Preparation

- newspaper
- tweezers
- scoop
- soil
- pot
- akadama soil
- fertilizer

1 Choose a slightly larger pot than the one in which the plant was previously planted.

2 Hover the plant to be replanted in the container and visualize its position.

3 Fill the pot about ⅓ full with akadama soil

4 Add enough soil to cover the akadama soil, and add a pinch of fertilizer.

5 Place the plant in the pot and check its height. If it is too low, add soil to adjust the height.

6 Once you are satisfied with the height, place the plant and add soil around it while holding it in place with one hand.

7 Once you've finished filling the pot with soil, hold the plant in place and lightly tap the pot to fill in the gaps. Add more soil to the pot to keep the balance.

8 Add decorative stones as desired.

9 Water the plant and you're done!

Diseases and Pests

Although succulents are easy to grow, they are often prone to disease and infestation. No matter how tough succulents are, disease and pests can cause them to wither and decay if left unchecked. Here we introduce some diseases and pests to watch out for and how to deal with them, from home remedies to commercial preparations (we mention just a few of the many available). Wear gloves and eye protection when using fungicides and insecticides. Carefully read and follow manufacturers' instructions for use and safety.

Diseases and Pests	Cause and Symptoms	What to do
Filamentous fungus	A thread fungus-like substance attaches to the plant and, if left unattended, will cause the plant to rot and wither. This fungus invades when the soil is too moist or poorly ventilated.	Remove the fungus-attached parts of the plant, rinse with water, and dry thoroughly. Spray with a copper, sulfur or neem oil-based fungicide.
Black rot	The stem and base of the plant turns black, becomes soft, and the rot gradually spreads. Black spots appear on leaves and stems.	Remove discolored areas and dry. Spray with a copper, sulfur or neem oil-based fungicide.
Black spot	Black spots appear on the leaves and stems, spreading and looking moldy. Infection occurs when the soil is weak or left in a poorly-ventilated area.	If symptoms are severe, discard the plants as they will infect other plants. If symptoms are mild, spray with a copper, sulfur or neem oil-based fungicide. Remove discolored parts and allow to dry.
Root rot/red rot	Stems and roots turn brown, soften and spread gradually. This can occur if the plant is left in a poorly ventilated area or not replanted for several years.	Remove discolored areas and dry. Spray with a copper, sulfur or neem oil-based fungicide
Red mites	Reddish insects about 0.5 mm in length. They attach to the plant and suck the juice, preventing growth and transmitting pathogens. The damaged area turns brownish.	Catch and kill as soon as found. May respond to a dish soap and water solution or insecticidal soap spray. Neem oil and sprays such as Bonide Mite-X are also effective.
Aphids	Small green or black insects 1–2 mm long. Swarms on young stems, leaves and shoots, sucking juices and stunting growth. Carrier of pathogens.	Catch and kill as soon as found. Rubbing alcohol (70%); a solution of dish soap, cooking oil and water; and a neem oil-based spray are all solutions for aphids. Be sure to get treatment into the nooks and crevices.
Silkworms	About 1.5 mm long. Attaches to plants, sucks juices, interferes with growth, and transmits disease-causing organisms.	Catch and kill as soon as found. Spray with a pesticide such as Garden Safe Bt Worm & Caterpillar or Monterey B.t.
Mealybug	The larva is about 2 mm long and the adult is covered with threads. The larvae are about 2 mm in length, and the adults are covered with threads.	Catch and kill as soon as found. Try rubbing alcohol (70%); a solution of dish soap and water, insecticidal soap; or one of the many systemic insecticides available on the market.
Slugs	The larvae are small, less than 1 mm long, and are covered with threads.	Catch and kill as soon as found. Use a slugicide if infested. You can also try natural deterrents such as eggshells or coffee grounds on the soil.
Root-knot nematode	Very small insects, less than 1 mm. They penetrate the roots and absorb nutrients. Cause unexplained, stunted growth above ground. Forms bumps on roots.	Cut off any roots that have bumps. Try a preparation such as Monterey Nematode Control.
Threadworms	White powdery mildew, about 1 mm long. Attach to roots and suck juice, preventing growth. They also transmit pathogens.	Wash roots with water when dividing plants. Spray with a pesticide such as Garden Safe Bt Worm & Caterpillar or Monterey B.t.
Red spider mite	Insects about 0.5 mm long. There are various types, including those that emit threads. Attach to plants, suck juice, prevent growth, and transmit pathogens.	Catch and kill as soon as found. Spray with a solution that targets mites, such as Bayer's BioAdvanced 3-In-1 Insect, Disease and Mite Control.
Armyworm	They are found in the soil during the daytime and hide at night.	Catch and kill as soon as they are found. Spray with a pesticide such as Garden Safe Bt Worm & Caterpillar or Monterey B.t.

The Fall Colors of Succulents

Fall is a time of year when the leaves of plants turn red. In fact, succulents also have fall foliage. Just like other plants succulents grow green until summer then change their foliage colors as the temperature drops rapidly toward winter. They may turn red or have a gradation of light pinks and greens, making them look even prettier than usual. The beautiful colors are so striking that you may forget that they are plants at all. The foliage of succulents changes from around November to March. Let's enjoy the beautiful foliage of your succulents by exposing them to the sun.

In order to get beautiful foliage...

The key to beautiful foliage is exposure to plenty of sunlight. Succulents, in general, love sunlight, so exposing them as much as possible will give you the best color these plants have to offer. If you keep them indoors with little sunlight, they will stay green. Another trick is to water a succulent only when the leaves are wrinkled and the soil is dry. If you put too much water in a container that has no drainage, it may cause root rot. In summer, water during cooler hours such as morning and evening, and in winter, it's best to water during warmer periods when the sun is shining.

Echeveria 'Debbie'

Echeveria purpusorum

Echeveria 'Mebina'

Graptoveria 'A Grim One'

Pechyphytum Oviferum 'Momobijin'

Echeveria 'pulidonis'

Pachyphytum longifolium

Echeveria chihuahuaensis

Echeveria 'Akinoshimo'

Echeveria 'Hanaikada'

Echeveria 'Peach Pride'

Echeveria derenbergii

The Succulents

Not all varieties have cute, plump leaves. Sometimes you'll look at a plant and ask, "Can this really be a succulent?" There are probably many more varieties of succulents than you've heard of or imagined. They look different from each other and grow in different cycles. Techniques for growing them also differ. So let's study the characteristics of each genus and how to grow them.

In the field guide pages, the cycle for each succulent is indicated by the following icons. The number in the pot represents the month. Please use these notations as a reference.

| Dormant season | Growth season | Blooming season | Peak viewing season |

Poellnitzianus Long, narrow, yellow-green leaves. Stem covered with brown hairs. A woody species.

Adromischus

Small, refined, loves sunlight.

Country of origin: South Africa
How to propagate: Leaf cutting, beheading

The leaves tend to fall off easily, but they often sprout from the fallen leaves, so they can multiply easily. There are many varieties showing diverse features, from hairy stems to mysterious patterns on the leaves. Many of these varieties are small and grow slowly—great for those who want a compact collection.

| 1 | 2 | 3 | 4 | 5 | 6 | 7 | 8 | 9 | 10 | 11 | 12 |

※ **Growing season is during cooler months**

Growing Tip

It is sensitive to heat, so it should be kept in the shade with good ventilation during the summer. However, it can easily survive the summer if it is watered sparingly. It grows well in cooler/cold weather. It doesn't need much water during the dormant season, but water it well during the growing season.

Triginas
Leaves have a mottled pattern and are reddish throughout the year. The color is stronger in strong sunlight.

Cristatus
Unique with its shaggy stems and fringed leaf edges. It will grow into a grove.

Hakutou
Transparent green leaves. Flowers well and beautifully. Weak in summer.

Matsumushi
The shoots turn reddish and produce dense, firm, thick leaves.

Aeonium (Tree House Leek)

The leaves look like flowers. Its presence is enhanced when it stands alone in a container.

Country of origin: North Africa
How to propagate: Beheading

With the leaves slowly withering from bottom to top, it creates a unique shape in which leaves live only at the tip. The leaves come in a variety of colors and patterns, and the patterns on the stems where the leaves have fallen are also interesting. There are many varieties, including large and small species. The stem wilts after flowering. It can be easily propagated by beheading.

※ **Growing period is during cold seasons**
※ **Flowering period is around March, but the shaft dies after flowering.**

Growing Tip

It does not tolerate extreme heat or cold well, so during the dormant season, the leaves drop and the plant looks a bit stark. In midsummer, keep it in a shady, well-ventilated area and water it sparingly to allow it to go dormant. However, at the beginning of the growing season in spring and fall, it shows excellent growth. It should be kept outdoors during the growing season, as it is sensitive to lack of sunlight.

Arboreum
The leaves have a deep color and grow to a fairly large size. Turns green in low light.

Aeonium
Small species, but when mature it becomes woody and looks like a small tree. Leaves are sticky and rest in summer.

Tricolor
Green with beautiful pink and yellow color from spring to fall. Naturally well branched to become a fine plant.

Sunburst
A species with beautiful outer leaf spots. It grows more slowly and slowly than other species. It does not branch much.

Clockwise from top left
Fukiage (a.k.a. Striata) /
'Kissho Kan' / Raijin

Agave

Beautifully formed rosette-like spreading, spiky leaves.

Country of origin: U.S.A., Mexico
How to propagate: Root division

It is a relatively long-lived species, with flowering ages ranging from 20 to nearly 100 years, but it flowers only once in its lifetime. After flowering, the mother plant dies and only the surrounding plantlets survive. This genus is famous for being used to make tequila. The leaves have spines at the tips, so be careful when handling them.

Growing Tip

Most varieties can be kept outdoors in summer and brought indoors only in winter. They have large water tanks and need less watering than other genuses. The lower leaves die first, but they can be easily removed by inserting a blade from the tip to the center of the leaf and tearing the leaf with force.

1 2 3 4 5 6 7 8 9 10 11 12

※ **Growing period is during hotter months.**
※ **Flowering period is mainly in summer, but the flower stems live for about one year.**

'Sakura-fubuki'

Anacampseros

Loved for its pastel gradation.

Country of origin: South Africa
How to propagate: Leaf cutting, beheading

When it flowers, it self-pollinates and produces fruits, and the seeds spill over and multiply naturally. You can propagate it by leaf cutting and beheading. It is fun to grow small buds, and there are many varieties with beautiful flowers. The flowers are large, which is hard to imagine from the size of the plant's body. The stems are characterized by a few white hairs.

Growing Tip

It is very tolerant of the cold and will grow well if you repot it twice a year. If you want it to grow quickly then repot it more often. Variegations are weak and slow-growing, so you can raise them slowly. Expose it to light and water it when the leaves begin to wrinkle.

※ **Flowering period is unpredictable.**

Aloe

There are many varieties and they are fun and easy to grow.

Country of origin: South Africa
How to propagate: Beheading, root division

This genus ranges from small, palm-sized trees to large varieties that grow to more than a foot tall. There are also two types: the grove variety, which grows upward as the lower leaves die back, and the clump variety, which produces many new plantlets and grows in clusters. Be careful to not damage the leaves. The juices will seep out and turn black which can result in rotting.

```
1  2  3  4  5  6  7  8  9  10  11  12
```

※ **Growing period is during cold seasons**
※ **Flowering is mainly from January to May, but depends on the variety.**

Growing Tip

Growing is easy, as most of them are generally hardy. It can survive without much water, but the tips of the leaves may wither and not grow beautifully. You can easily increase the number of shoots by beheading it, but it is best to avoid forcibly picking the plantlets* for propagation during hot weather. (*The process of removing the growing point at the tip of the stem to increase the number of shoots.)

Tiger Tooth
Tiger Tooth Aloe's yellowish foliage is more pigmented in colder months. It grows in groves. Be careful, as it is sensitive to cold.

Vera
The most popular aloe. When small in size, it looks as pictured here. Easy to grow, resistant to cold and heat. Super snowy, beautiful pink foliage. It grows in a magnificent clump with its young out to the side.

'Marsha Layhew'
Place some pups near each other and grow a beautiful colony.

Hybrid
Hybrid of *Descoingsii* and *Haworthiodes*. Beautiful compact rosette with fine leaf stipules. Small species.

Brevifolia
Beautiful blue color. Turns slightly pink in full sun. It does not grow tall and forms a large rosette.

Variegata
Beautifully spotted foliage with very thick-walled leaves that develop into a firm rosette. Flowers easily.

From top
Little Prince / Shukuten / Treasured Palace / Hatobue

Conophytum

A mysterious succulent that looks like teeth.

Country of origin: South Africa
How to propagate: Leaf cutting, sowing seed

During the dormant season, the plant is covered with withered bark and appears to be dead. When it wakes from dormancy it sheds its dead skin and flowers will appear. Plants that flowered once in the previous year divide into two heads, and those that flowered twice divide into three heads. Those that did not flower do not divide and produce only one head. The flowers of each variety are fixed.

Growing Tip

Water them during the growing season, and let them rest during the dormant season. For faster growth, you can repot it in September. Repotting is a good time to divide the plants for propagation. When you divide them, be sure not to damage the stems. It is best always to expose the plant to light while it is growing.

Namaquensis

Albuca
Succulent with curly leaf tips.

Country of origin: South Africa
How to propagate: Root division

All *Albuca* species grow from bulbs, and there are many interesting varieties, such as *Albuca spiralis*. It produces flowers during spring, and these can be either upright or pendulous.

Growing Tip

Since the growing season is in spring, replanting should be done from around winter to early spring. This genus is easy to grow and tolerates both cold and heat. Expose it to full sun throughout the year. Water the plants well during the growing season and avoid watering during the dormant season.

※ **It goes dormant in midsummer.**

Climbing Onion

Bowiea
Looks like a vine growing out of an onion.

Country of origin: South Africa
How to propagate: Root division

Like an onion, this plant is only a bulb during the dormant winter season, and asparagus-like vines grow in the spring. The propagation method is different: divide the ball into four pieces, peel off one scale piece at a time, and insert each piece into the soil to produce offspring. This is a difficult method so it's not recommended for beginners.

Growing Tip

Water only when the plant has leaves, and very little watering is needed when the bulb is dormant. Water well in the growing season to grow the bulb. If the bulb is small, its water storage capacity is low, so water it more frequently.

Fagaroides

Brucella

Is this really a succulent? Yes. It's a succulent characterized by the fragrance of its leaves.

Country of origin: North Africa
How to propagate: Beheading

The genus is very tolerant of drought when the plant has leaves. The trunk is thick and the bark peels off to reveal a smooth skin like that of a baobab. The leaves also have a peppery fragrance. During the dormant season, all the leaves fall off, and during the growing season, new shoots emerge and grow.

Growing Tip

During summer, it should be treated like a normal tree. During the frost-free season, it grows well when planted outdoors. Before the frost, take it up and move it into your house or greenhouse, and leave it alone, unplanted, until spring. If planted in pots, you should refrain from watering to keep it under control.

String of Hearts

Ceropegia

The leaf patterns and the flowers are
quite unique!

Country of origin: South Africa
How to propagate: Saproot

The leaves are very small, which is the charm of this
variety. The trunk is the main source of photosynthesis, so be sure to keep it well-exposed to light.
Ceropegia is a vine, and its leaf pattern is unique, as
is the shape of the flower. Even beginners can easily
get it to bloom. *Ceropegia woodii f.variegata* (String of
Hearts) is one of the most famous varieties.

Growing Tip

Most of the varieties are summer type, but the vine type
does better in a little shade. It has a bulb, from which the
vine grows. Replant this bulb if you want more vines. You
may want to water it a little during the growing season. Even
during the dormant period, if you give a small amount of
water (that is, do not completely stop watering during this
time), you can prevent it from withering.

※ **Flowering period may vary slightly depending on the variety.**

26

Elephantipes

Dioscorea
Vines grow out of a turtle's shell!

Country of origin: North Africa
How to propagate: Sow seeds

The bulb part looks like a turtle's shell, but the vine and leaves are very similar to yam. The interesting pattern on the bulb part makes it a popular variety. It grows slowly, so mature plants are expensive to buy. There are American and Mexican varieties, and the growth cycles are the exact opposite, so keep that in mind when purchasing and planting.

Growing Tip

It should be grown only during the leafy season whenever the soil is dry (but do not allow the plant to sit in an excess of water). The vines grow too long, so wrapping them around a support pole saves space. However, keeping the foliage as thick as possible will encourage growth in the following years, so do not cut the vines even if they are in the way.

Grown in U.S.A.

| 1 | 2 | 3 | 4 | 5 | 6 | 7 | 8 | 9 | 10 | 11 | 12 |

Grown in Mexico

| 1 | 2 | 3 | 4 | 5 | 6 | 7 | 8 | 9 | 10 | 11 | 12 |

27

Cotyledon
Lovely plump, fleshy leaves.

Country of origin: South Africa
How to propagate: Beheading

When viewed from above, the leaves seem to form a cross shape. Each time a new leaf emerges, it rotates 90 degrees and emerges alternately. Kalanchoe flowers also have a cross shape (four petals), whereas cotyledon flowers have five petals and are pentagonal in shape. Cotyledon flowers are very large and spectacular, and they are also very easy to bloom.

| 1 | 2 | 3 | 4 | 5 | 6 | 7 | 8 | 9 | 10 | 11 | 12 |

※ Flowering period may vary slightly depending on the variety.

Growing Tip

Although it is one of the easiest plants to grow in the stonecrops family, recently produced varieties seem to be susceptible to heat. There are many varieties that are tolerant of cold and can survive the winter outdoors. The varieties with white powder on them prefer full sun so make sure they are exposed to sunlight.

Ladismithiensis (Kitten's Claw)
Named after the shape of the leaves, which resemble a cat's claws. The leaves are long and narrow and small. The leaf has three claws on its edge, compared to five on Kumadojis.

Orbirulata
White powdery foliage with beautiful purplish-red edges. It grows tall and stands straight up.

Kumadoji (Bear Cub)
This one is called 'kumadoji' because it looks like a bear cub holding its hands together. The entire body is covered with fur, which is fluffy and thick.

Undulata
The fringe of the leaves looks like waves. Its pure white, powdery leaves make it stand out. It grows into a large tree.

Fukkura
The leaves are round and covered with white powder. Only the edges turn red during fall. A small species that grows in clumps.

Crassula (Pigmyweed)

Unique appearance with stunning fall foliage.

Country of origin: South Africa, East Africa
How to propagate: Beheading

Most varieties have cross-forming leaves like the Kalanchoe and the Cotyledon, but this one is more square. The flowers are five-petaled and fragrant. There are many varieties of this genus, and within them, many variations, making Crassula a fine genus to collect. Many varieties have beautiful fall foliage.

※ **Flowering period depends on each variety.**

Growing Tip

Most of them are weak in summer, so try to grow them during winter. During summer, place them in a well-ventilated place and refrain from watering. For ventilation, you can even use a fan to blow air through the plants. It is better to keep them on a balcony and shield them from light, rather than placing them in a closed room in the summer. Propagate in fall rather than spring due to sensitivity to humidity.

Ramota
The surface is covered with hairs. It grows by creeping and spreading and has small leaves, like a vine. When the colors start changing during fall, the leaves turn a beautiful purple.

Brevifolia
Grows with thick, tightly spaced leaves. The edges of the leaves turn red during fall foliage.

Watermeyeri
The leaves turn a beautiful reddish hue during fall. The leaf surface is covered with hairs. Flowers grow and bloom well.

Rupestris
They have very fleshy leaves that are pale green with yellowish edges. The growth is slow, but the bright foliage makes it ideal for group planting.

'Springtime'
It has beautiful pink flowers rising out of firm, deep green foliage. Popular for its easy flowering.

cv. Flame
It's green in the warmer months, and bright red during fall! The bright red color is gorgeous in group plantings. This variety likes sunlight.

'Ivory Pagoda'
The surface has a unique feathery texture. Growth is slow, but the plantlets generally start growing on the sides forming clusters.

Also called the propeller plant because of the shape and arrangement of its leaves. If you let it dry between waterings, it will have a fresher texture.

'Morgan's Beauty'
It's a small species that grows very slowly. In early spring it produces beautiful pink flowers with a hydrangea-like center.

'Campfire'
Leaves are rather flame-shaped, and the name becomes even more apt when they change color in fall. The pink color becomes more intense and more spectacular.

Perforata
Its pink-tinged leaves are less fleshy than those of many other species. Grows upright and produces lovely flower clusters.

'Emerald'
This variety is not very tall and grows in clusters horizontally. The flowers have a slight odor and are very fertile.

Pubescens
The small, hair-covered leaves are easily detached making them very easy to propagate through beheading. Small flowers bloom at the end of long necks. It does not do so well in summer humidity.

'Gollum'
This species is popular for its unique appearance and is often said to look like something extraterrestrial. It is a jade cultivar (page 33).

Dejecta
During fall foliage, the leaves turn yellow and red. It grows quickly, and if grown in a large pot, it will grow into a fine little shrub.

Rogersii
The round leaves are covered with tiny hair. They turn red during fall and back to green in warmer months. This plant grows in clusters.

Columella
The square leaves are unique in the way they are strung together to form a series of supporting branches. After growing upward, they fall down, sprout again and grow in clusters.

Hirsuta
Their thick, slender leaves develop into a rosette shape. When a new leaf emerges, it is rough and matte.

Tecta
These grow at a very slow pace. The leaves overlap neatly in a crisscross pattern. The leaf surface bears a pattern. Its flower blooms out from the center.

Ovata
This is a popular species that has been around for a long time. When it grows large, the stem thickens firmly and it looks like a mature tree.

'Benichigo'
In the warmer months, its leaves are green and small, making it look like a weed, but when the leaves turn red and the flowers bloom, it attracts attention.

Sarmentosa
Beautifully spotted leaves. The stem turns solid red during fall which contrasts beautifully with the leaves turning yellow.

Little Falcata
A small species of the *falcata*. Its small overlapping leaves spread to the right and left. The flower head extends upward and the appearance of the bloom is quite picturesque.

33

Echeveria
Beautiful leaves that bloom like a flower.

Country of origin: Africa, Central and South America
How to propagate: Leaf sprouting, beheading

There are many varieties, but they can be roughly divided into two types: the large cabbage type and the thick-fleshed rosette type. The leaves of the rosette type are easy to pinch, but this method isn't feasible for cabbage types. So once the stem has grown to a certain length for the cabbage type, you'll need to behead the plant and then plant the cutting. The beheaded stem can be used for propagation, as babies can sprout from it.

| 1 | 2 | 3 | 4 | 5 | 6 | 7 | 8 | 9 | 10 | 11 | 12 |

※ It rarely goes dormant, but it is sensitive to heat, so it is better to avoid watering it during summer to give it a rest.
※ Flowering period is irregular throughout the year.

Growing Tip
Keep it in a well-lit area but avoid direct sunlight in summer. Since it grows quickly and the lower leaves wilt one after another, the dead leaves may become moldy and eventually kill the entire plant if they are not removed frequently. In summer it is adverse to humidity, so ventilate it well and avoid watering.

'Wild Rose'
It's a delicate variety, with only the tips of the leaves turning red. Similar to the *derenbergii* but this one is a little larger. It is sensitive to humidity.

'Panda'
The leaves become firmly puffed up around fall, and at this time the pink tinge is most pronounced. It is susceptible to humidity.

'Hakuhou'
The broad leaves of this variety can vary from green to yellow, even orange. It prefers full sun and is weak against cold temperatures. In the spring it produces orange flowers.

'Bombycina'
The leaves and stem are covered with tiny hairs. When the leaves change color during fall, the entire plant turns slightly red. It is susceptible to humidity.

Pallida
During fall, it turns a bright, almost yellow color. A woody species, the leaves at the bottom wilt, and only the top buds form a rosette.

'Pinky'
This little guy has beautiful pink, lightly powdery foliage. It is very susceptible to humidity. It's best to let the soil dry out between waterings.

Derenbergii
Small and withered in summer, but grows quickly in fall and winter. It is sensitive to humidity, so avoid watering during summer.

'Perle Von Nurnberg'
This variety has a nice pink color all year round. It's an elegant species with beautifully shaped leaves.

Kesselringii
This variety has a beautiful pale green color. It grows into a small rosette of fleshy leaves. Generally a small species. It goes dormant during summer.

'Tatsuta'
The angular shapes of the leaves are impressive. Grows slowly and is susceptible to humidity. It has very beautiful tints of red during fall. This species grows in clusters

Pulidonis
The leaves are slender and elegant. When the leaves change color during fall, they turn bright red toward the tips. This species grows in clusters. Also known under the scientific name *hamsii*.

'A Grim One'
Popular for its light, gentle pink foliage. It also flowers well. It does not like summer humidity, so make sure it doesn't get overheated during summer.

Chihuahuaensis
This is a small species. Leaves turn strong colors toward the tips. Popular for its small, compact form. This one is also sensitive to humidity.

Tolimanensis
The entire plant is covered with white powder and the tips of the leaves are very sharp. When the leaves change color during fall, the entire plant turns pink. It grows at a slow pace.

Yamatobini
The leaves are patterned and turn red during fall. This species is similar to, *Yamato Nishiki*, but with thinner leaves.

'Spruce Oliver'

A grove, spreading rosette-like leaves only on the upper part of the tree. The leaves are lightly hairy. Growth is slow.

'Olivia'

A stump-forming species, where the lower leaves die off in turn and grow upward. During fall, the leaves change color to a gradation from red to pink.

'Golden Fire'

This variety has a beautiful pale pink color. It develops a large rosette and does not grow tall. It grows at a slow pace.

'Lipstick'

A woody species. It grows into a large rosette, turning bright red during fall. In warmer months, the leaves are green and smaller.

Bicolor

A woody species. The rosette is not large but the stem grows tall. The leaves turn a light shade of red during fall.

Elegans

Its signature blue-green leaves turn pale pink during fall. They do not grow tall, but become large rosettes.

'Lola'

This variety has an elegant leaf shape. Leaf edges turn bright pink during fall. Be careful of humidity.

'Briar Rose'

A woody species. The lower leaves witter in order and grow upward. During foliage season, they are almost reddish pink.

Supia

A woody species that remains small. The leaves turn a beautiful red.

Euphorbia (Spurges)

Lots of unique varieties—you'll want to collect them!

Country of origin: Africa, Madagascar
How to propagate: Sow seeds or beheading

The sap of most varieties is toxic, so be careful not to get it on mucous membranes. When handling them, wear gloves and avoid touching your eyes. Some varieties have both male and female plants, and many of them have small flowers and leaves, giving them a unique appearance.

※ **Flowering time may differ slightly from variety to variety.**

Growing Tip

Too-high temperatures can weaken the plant. It is best to avoid cutting back or replanting in mid-summer. When you cut the buds, sap milky sap will seep out. Soak the cut end in a little water to let the sap run off and let it dry a few to several days, away from direct sunlight, before placing in a well-draining soil medium. It takes longer to sprout than other genuses, so be patient.

Obesa
Grows into a round ball with a plaid-like surface pattern. As it grows larger, it grows upward into a more spherical shape.

Horrida
Characterized by its surface pattern. Thorns remain on the stem of the flower. The flower stalk turns red during the growing season.

Enopla
The green color contrasts beautifully with the red thorns. To keep the pretty red color, avoid overwatering.

Susannae
It's deep green with a unique shape. It blooms a yellow flower from the center.

Trigona
A very popular hybrid as an interior cactus. It produces leaves only during the growing season.

Milii
It sprouts leaves during the growing season but defoliates in winter. Flowers bloom well for this variety.

'Bronze'

Graptopetalum (Leatherpetal)

A fun succulent that can be propagated quickly.

Country of origin: Mexico
How to propagate: Leaf cutting, beheading

Most of them are hardy, except for a few varieties. It is a genus with a strong life force. Most of the varieties can be propagated through leaf cuttings. The beautiful pinkish-red foliage can be enjoyed in all varieties.

Growing Tip

This genus is resistant to both cold and heat making it easy to raise. There are varieties that can be grown outdoors year-round, such as the *paraguayense* (Ghost Plant) variant. It grows quickly and propagates as if it were sprawling over the ground. If you grow it in a lot of sunlight, it will produce beautiful fall foliage. If it grows too large, you can behead it and plant the cutting to make it more compact.

※ **Goes dormant around mid-summer**

Leucotricha

Sinningia
Lovely velvety leaves.

Country of origin: Brazil
How to propagate: Leaf cutting by cutting the leaf at the stem and drying it until a callous forms at the cut

Flowers emerge before or at the same time as the leaves once it awakens from dormancy, around April. While leaf shape and flower color vary, the leaves are velvety and the flowers are trumpet-shaped. It is native to Brazil; the *Sinningia leucotricha* is also called "Brazilian Edelweiss."

Growing Tip

During the dormant season, the plant is only a bulb, so avoid intense light and allow it to rest. Although it is a bulbous plant, it should be kept watered as long as it has leaves. Even during the dormant period in summer, it is good to cover the topsoil with Sphagnum moss to keep it from drying out too much. When the leaves fall off, do not assume the plant has died, but keep an eye on it until it reaches its growth stage. When small sprouts begin to appear, the plant is ready to grow. Resume watering at this stage.

From left to right
Aranami / Trigana

Faucaria

Looking like a waiting animal's open mouth, this plant is impressive from every angle.

Country of origin: South Africa
How to propagate: Seed sowing, beheading

This genus is often called "Tiger Jaws" for its spiny leaf edges. There are many varieties, but they are almost all similar in shape. There are white-flowered and yellow-flowered varieties. Flowers need a few hours of direct sunlight to bloom, opening in the afternoon and closing in the evening.

Growing Tip

It is very hardy and can be grown outdoors except during the coldest season. However, it grows quickly, so it is best to replant frequently, even annually. If the plant is well-exposed to light, it will flower well and keep its beautiful appearance. You can increase the number of plants by dividing them.

※ **Flowering time may differ slightly depending on the variety.**

Aurantiaca

Fenestraria

Lens mechanism at the pip of the stick-like leaf.

Country of origin: South Africa
How to propagate: Division

The scientific name *Fenestraria* means "window," and indeed the tip of the leaf has a lens shape similar to a skylight. They are called "Baby Toes" for the leaves' cylindrical shape and clump-like formation. They produce lovely white or yellow flowers in spring and fall.

Growing Tip

Its growing period is most of the year and tends to grow in clumps. The plants are tender, so if they grow too thickly, they may rot inside, and eventually die. Regardless of the season, propagate it when it grows large, or if you do not want to increase the number of plants, then water it moderately. It does not tolerate humidity, so it will lose its form during the summer, but it will grow from the fall with a strong increase in foliage.

1 2 3 4 5 6 7 8 9 10 11 12

※ **Flowering time may vary slightly from variety to variety.**

Gasteria

Firm, fleshy, textured leaves.

Country of origin: South America
How to propagate: Root division

This genus is nicknamed "Ox Tongue" because if its leaf shape. The leaves overlap in two directions. If grown in humid conditions and kept from dropping the lower leaves, it will grow into a five-story pagoda-like plant. The leaves are thick, tough and textured. Species in this genus range from small to large. It can be easily multiplied by dividing the plant.

| 1 | 2 | 3 | 4 | 5 | 6 | 7 | 8 | 9 | 10 | 11 | 12 |

※ **It goes dormant when it gets too hot in midsummer.**

Growing Tip

Although it grows year-round, it may develop root rot if it is not repotted regularly. It is best to replant once a year. To ensure good growth, give it as much sunlight as possible, but be careful—if the sun is too strong, the plant will burn, so adjust accordingly.

Maculata
This one looks a little like a cow tongue. It has rough textured leaves developed on both sides. It grows at a slow pace.

Pillansii
This variety's matte, fleshy, rounded leaves develop on both sides. It grows at a slow pace.

Gracilis var. minima
This variety is a small species. It produces many offspring and grows in clusters.

Dicta
This variety has slightly grayish matte leaves. As with some other varieties, leaves can be pointed or somewhat rounded on the same plant.

'Ginsha-Kodakara'
It has whitish, matte-textured leaves. When the leaves are larger they form a rosette.

Glomerata
The deep gray-green leaves are fleshy, irregular and have a rough, uneven texture.

From top left
Fulleri / Lesliei /
Pseudotruncatella
Lesliei / Aucampiae /
Pseudotruncatella
Aucampiae / Lesliei /
Pseudotruncatella

Lithops (Living Stone)

A plant that mimics stones to protect itself from being eaten. It also molts!

Country of origin: South Africa
How to propagate: Sow seeds or shoots

Like Fenestraria (page 43), this variety produces sky-lights that have a variety of patterns on them. There are many species with variations in color and shape. It is an animal-like plant that changes its structure by molting once a year, possibly more than once.

Growing Tip

Since it is sensitive to summer heat and humidity, keep it as cool as possible in a well-ventilated spot. You can even use a fan for ventilation. The growing season is from fall to spring. Water well during the growing season to keep the plants plump. During the summer months, avoid watering and allow the plants to rest. If they do not get enough light, they will stretch and weaken and eventually die.

Albiflos

Haemanthus

A bulbous genus of infinite variety.

Country of origin: South Africa
How to propagate: Root division

Leaves vary in number (as few as one or as many as six), in texture (from smooth to leathery or sticky) and shape (from the prone, rounded leaves you see here to slender and erect). The flowers also vary, from somewhat trumpet-like to bushy in shape, and from white to fiery in color.

Growing Tip

As with *higanbana*, most of them bloom in fall and go dormant in summer, leaving only the bulbs, so try to grow them during winter. When the leaves wither, remove them with scissors.

※ **During the dormant season, the leaves of the blood-lily and Crispus varieties fall off and only the flower remains.**

Haworthia

Many species have lens-like structures at the tips of their leaves.

Country of origin: South Africa
How to propagate: Root division

This is an advanced genus that has a lens-like structure at the tip of the leaf, which collects light and takes it into the body. The transparency of the leaf tips is one of its many charms. It is a popular genus among succulent lovers, and many hybrids have been created crossing *Haworthia* with other genuses, resulting in plants with distinct characteristics from both families.

Growing Tip

Grow in soft light rather than strong light. If this is hard to gauge, adjust the light and watering according to the plant's condition. If the leaves turn brown, there is too little water or the sun is too strong (or both). If the leaves grow longer than they should, there is either too much water or not enough light. Hardier leaf types are more resilient. You can water them year round.

Fasciata 'Super White'
This variety has broader white bands than *fasciata*. At home indoors or out—even planted in the ground.

Shizukuishi
This one has lenses at the tips of the leaves. The leaves are beautifully translucent and rounded.

'Kyo no Mai'
Beautiful yellow-green leaves. The leaf tips are a little translucent.

Obtusa
If exposed to strong light and fertilized only lightly, it will appear to have reddish foliage.

'Shizuko'
A hybrid of the *truncata*. The tips of the leaves are thinner than those of the *truncata* and grow in a rosette shape.

Kaffirdriftensis
The leaves are thin and short with a pattern of pure white dots. Tolerance to low light makes this a good indoor plant.

Fasciata Variegata
This one is notable for its spots. The yellow and white color creates a bright variation on *fasciata*. It can be used as an accent in a group planting.

Luteolosa
This one is a small species. It is popular for its compact grassy appearance.

Umbraticola
A small species popular for its rounded leaf tips and bright green color. Produces plantlets often and grows in clusters.

Cuspidata
The leaves form into rosettes. Their surface is translucent.

Turgita
Leaves are bright green, and their surface has a smoother texture than most others.

Retusa
The leaves are long and flat. It has lenses at the leaf tips.

Attenuata
The leaves are thicker than the *fasciata* variety and it has a mottled pattern. The leaves turn red when it's exposed to cold.

Fasciata
Now called *Haworthiopsis fasciata*, this is popular variety is great for beginners and does well indoors.

Astroloba
The bright green leaves have a mottled pattern and grow pointing upwards.

'Kakyo'
Grows in a compact rosette with small leaves. It produces plantlets often and grows in clusters.

Mantellii
Has deep green leaves with lenses at the leaf tips. This one is a hybrid species.

Helmae
Leaves are a bright yellowish green, a little translucent at the tips.

Obtusa hybrids
Leaves are generally round, plump and richly colored.

Splendens
Unique appearance with reptile-like texture and coloration and a unique surface pattern.

Bolusii
The tips of the leaves are lacy and form large, beautiful rosettes. Grows slowly.

Lens Structure

Among the varieties of *Haworthia*, there are two main types of leaves: soft and hard. As you become acquainted with these plants you'll notice that most of the soft types have a transparent lens at the tips of their leaves. This leaf structure makes sense when you know the origin of the *Haworthia*. Normally, a plant's body grows above ground and the plant takes in sun through its entire body. However, because some species are native to regions with high heat and little rainfall, if they reach maturity in the way of common plants they face huge disadvantages. Water will evaporate too quickly for them to take it in, and water-thirsty animals will seek them out. For protection, these plants' bodies remain mostly underground. This, of course, is not optimal for photosynthesis, but the lens allows them to take in sufficient light. Conversely, outside of desert habitats, it is difficult to grow these plants as they're grown in the wild, as there's too little sunlight and too much humidity. Not only some species of *Haworthia*, but also *Lithops* and *Fenestraria* have lenses.

Tartogo

Jatropha (Nettlespurges)

Beautiful coral-like flowers. The leaves are also big and powerful!

Country of origin: Central and South America
How to propagate: Seedling

If you are an experienced grower, you can grow the trunk into the shape shown in the photo in just one year after planting. During the growing season, it produces large leaves and orange flowers that resemble coral. It is popular as interior decor because of its fast growth and large, unique grass form.

Growing Tip

Since it is a completely tropical plant, it needs a minimum temperature of 59°F (15°C), but recent varieties can tolerate winter at around 41°F (5°C). If this temperature is still too cold for your plant, cut off the leaves and flowers before frost arrives, then leave the plant dry while it goes dormant until spring. Water frequently during the growing season.

※ **It is extremely susceptible to cold.**

53

Kalanchoe
So many charming and unusual species!

Country of origin: Madagascar, South Africa
How to propagate: Leaf cutting, beheading

Many varieties have extremely fertile leaves from which flowers sprout. Some varieties are named "pinnata" because they can reproduce by expelling many plantlets from the edge of the leaf. There are many varieties with patterned leaves, hairy leaves, and other unique varieties that are fun to collect.

| 1 | 2 | 3 | 4 | 5 | 6 | 7 | 8 | 9 | 10 | 11 | 12 |

※ **Growing period is almost throughout the year, but they are not so tolerant of extreme heat and cold.**
※ **Flowering time varies greatly depending on the species.**

Growing Tip

Most of them are summer type, but many of them bloom in winter, so keep them as warm as possible. When the temperature is warm enough, they thrive and can be grown like most non-succulent flowers and grasses, but in winter, they suddenly stop growing and rest. Be sure to bring them indoors before frost.

Humilis
Marbled pattern on leaf tips. Beautiful reddish color. It looks like a sea anemone.

Arborescens
A woody species. The leaves are round and fat in winter, and the edges of the leaves turn red.

Hildebrandtii
An erect, woody plant that often shares the common name "Silver Spoons" with *Kalanchoe Bracteata*.

Beharensis
Leaves and stems are covered with hair. The leaves wither from the bottom and the plant grows upward. A woody species.

Rhombopilosa
The leaves are silver with a brown speckled pattern. They are easily detached, making them easy to remove for leaf cuttings.

Black Tomentosa
Their unique feature s the brown blotches connecting to the black tips. It is a variety of the 'Tsuki Usagimimi' (page 56).

Tomentosa
The "Panda Plant" has variants depending on the color and shape of the leaves and the pattern of the brown markings.

Beharensis 'Fang'
The name "fang" is derived from the texture of the underside of the leaves. The entire plant is covered with hair.

Thyrsiflora
Its leaf is round like a red lotus and turns bright red in fall. This is a slow-growing plant.

Pinnata
This species bears many offspring at the edge of its leaves, which drop off and reproduce rapidly. It is also known by names such as "Miracle Leaf" and "Life Plant" as this plant plays a role in traditional medicine.

Orgyalis
Commonly called "Copper Spoons" for its ovate, richly-colored leaves. It produces beautiful trumpet-shaped yellow flowers in spring. Best to let soil dry out between waterings.

Kewensis
A unique species with a beautiful seaweed-like appearance. The shape of the leaves is interesting. It turns a beautiful red color in foliage season.

Eriophylla
Nicknamed 'Snow White' for the pure white hair that covers the entire leaf surface. It is sensitive to heat. Refrain from watering in summer.

Longiflora Coccinea
High-impact because of the edges and color (especially in fall) of its leaves. The species spreads as it grows.

Marnieriana
Grows large in a grove. Leaves with reddish margins. Grows quickly.

Rhombopilosa (Himeya)
An elegant variety that's brown and looks a little withered. It grows slowly into a grove.

Rotundifolia
The leaves come off rapidly, and it reproduces well. The pink color of the red leaves is beautiful and the flowers are cute.

'Fushicho'
Like the *Pinnata* variety, it breeds by producing many offspring at the edge of its leaves. The leaves are slender and serrated, very unique.

Grandiflora 'Fuyumomiji'
This is a Japanese variety whose name means "winter maple." The shell-shaped leaves turn a bright coral.

'Golden Girl'
A slower-growing variety of the *Tomentosa*. The name refers to the warmer tint of the leaves and softer brown of the markings.

Tomentosa 'Nousagi'
"Nousagi" translates as "wild rabbit." This variety is brownish color and has small leaves. Closely related to the 'Golden Girl' variety.

Ellenbeckii

Monadenium
Stem and leaves are smooth and elegant.

Country of origin: Tanzania
How to propagate: Beheading

This genus is similar to *Euphorbia* in nature and shape, though its flowers are primarily in cup-shaped clusters and come in a variety of colors. Stems vary depending on the species, from those that die in dormancy to those that produce new growth.
It produces leaves during the warm growing season, all of which are shed during the dormant period.

Growing Tip

They are similar to Euphorbias, but many of them are more susceptible to cold, so be especially careful when caring for them over winter. Always keep them indoors. In general, make sure they are well-watered (topsoil should not be completely dry). In winter, restrict watering to times when the stem seems about to wilt. When the weather warms up water more frequently to allow growth.

Bolusii

Pleiospilos

Like a dinosaur egg.

Country of origin: South Africa
How to propagate: Sow seeds

The most obvious characteristic of this genus is that it looks like an egg placed on its side. It grows and molts every year. While many other mesembs (mimicry plants) bloom in the fall, this genus blooms in early spring. The flower stalks are short and produce large dandelion-like flowers. There are many unusual varieties with unique forms, textures, and surface patterns.

Pleiospilos require well-drained soil and little water. A basic guideline is the feel of the leaves. If they've been feeling soft for a few days, it's a good time to water your plant. They like partial shade to full sun. When they're indoors, give them as much sun as possible. They are not cold-hardy, so in winter, this light is especially necessary.

Pachyphytum

An elegant variety of beauties.

Country of origin: Mexico
How to propagate: Leaf cutting, beheading

The leaves of this genus are especially fleshy. It can be easily propagated by leaf cuttings. Beheading is also an option; in fact, cutting and replanting is the best way to deal with plants that have grown too long. The root growth of the cutting will be slow, but the roots will grow quite strong.

| 1 | 2 | 3 | 4 | 5 | 6 | 7 | 8 | 9 | 10 | 11 | 12 |

※ **Flowering period may vary slightly from variety to variety.**

Growing Tip

It grows almost year-round, but can be replanted at any time. It is resistant to cold and heat, making it easy to care for. Because of its thick leaves, it grows a little slower than other members of the Stonecrop family, so it is recommended for those who want to take time growing it. It withers from the lower leaves and grows upwards. You can water it all year round. Make sure to expose it to full sun.

'Momobijin' (Peach Beauty)
Popular for its plump round leaves. It is a slow grower.

'Sakurabijin' (Cherry Blossom Beauty)
These plump leaves take on the hues of fall.

'Tsukibijin' (Moon Beauty)
The leaves are slightly elongated. In fall they turn purple, then red.

Longifolium
The leaves are firm, hardy, water-absorbing, and angular. When the leaves change color in fall, they turn purple-pink.

Compactum
Leaves look large, firm, dense and hardy.

'Mikaeri-Bijin' (Double Take Beauty)
The leaves are long and narrow and form a beautiful rosette. It grows quickly and is strong. It has a lovely pink color in fall.

Pilansii

Cheiridopsis
Leaves in amazing shapes.

Country of origin: South Africa
How to propagate: Sow seeds

This is a spring-flowering genus that blooms often over the course of the season and varies wonderfully both in the shape of its leaves—from fingers to hearts—and the colors and shapes of its flowers. It is easy to propagate by root dividing.

Growing Tip

It is easy to grow and can be replanted at any time. It prefers light, so always place it in the sun. In summer, it will continue to grow as long as it is well-ventilated.

From left
afra Variegata / Molokiniensis

Portulacaria

Plump stems and balanced form.

Country of origin: South Africa
How to propagate: Stem cuttings

Plants in this genus generally make good house plants. Unfortunately, they are not likely to flower unless/until they grow to a very large size. The leaves of the *Portulacaria afra* are edible. The *molokiniensis*, a native of Hawaii, becomes invasive if planted in the ground.

It is very easy to grow and will grow rapidly as long as it is kept watered. It is sensitive to cold, so it should be placed indoors during winter. If the leaves are wilted due to disease or some other reason, clean them off to prevent the disease from spreading. If there is a lack of sunlight, the leaves will fall off.

1 2 3 4 5 6 7 8 9 10 11 12

※ **Grows well in warmer temperatures, but will stop growing in colder temperatures.**

Sedum (Stonecrop)

A bubbly species with beautiful fall foliage.

Country of origin: Mexico
How to propagate: Leaf cutting, beheading

The Spanish Stonecrop is a typical variety that has beautiful red foliage in fall. It is popular for its thick-walled leaves as well as its color, small flowers and compact form. It grows well indoors or out. Outdoors, it spreads out, making lovely groundcover. Most species can tolerate poor soil and colder temperatures.

※ **Growing season: April to October (for crawling type);** standing plants grow all year long
※ **Dormancy: Winter (for crawling type)**

Growing Tip

Most varieties are tolerant to cold. Those that spread and grow like grass (sarmentosum) can be grown outdoors at all times. Taller varieties produce flowers. Sedum likes full sun and well-draining soil.

Dendroideum
Glossy, slender, firm, stiff leaves. A woody species that grows upward.

Praealtum
A round leaf type of dendroideum. During fall, the leaf edges take on a lovely red color.

Pedilanthus
A variant of the *allantoides*. This one has flatter leaves.

'Burrito'
The small round leaves are densely packed together like clusters of grapes. Grows in drooping clusters.

'Purple Haze'
Similar to Corsican. This variety is larger and has more beautiful foliage.

'Aurora' Variegata
Small and compact leaves. Red foliage. Beautiful and easy to bloom. Slightly susceptible to cold.

Pachyphyllum
Only the tips of the leaves turn red.
Beware of overheating in summer.

Corynephyllum
Leaves shaped like bananas. A woody species, the lower leaves wither and
grow upward.

Allantoides 'Goldii'
Beautiful blue color all year round. A
fast-growing upright species.

'Little Gem'
A small, slow-growing species. Leaves
are glossy and very compact.

Adolphi
Turns extra-yellow, during foliage
season, but its yellow leaves can be
enjoyed all year round.

Clavatum
Green leaves. During the foliage
season, the tips of the leaves turn red.
Grows at a fast pace.

'Corsican Stonecrop'
A collection of very small leaves. Grows in clusters. The front of the leaves is covered with hairs.

'Spanish Stonecrop'
The green leaves turn bright red in fall and winter. Tolerant to the cold. It grows quickly and is easy to grow outdoors.

Rubrotinctum
Glossy, deep green. Slow-growing, upright species.

'Golden Glow'
A spotted yellowish green. It has white spots and beautiful pinkish coloration during fall.

Milotteii
Rounded leaves, compact, upright growth. It is susceptible to summer humidity. It stops growing in summer.

'Aurora'
Spotted with rainbow dots. Its overall gray hue turns to beautiful pink during foliage season.

'Aurora Borealis'
Glossy yellow leaves all year round. A woody species. Slow-growing.

Treleasei
The leaves are rounded and it grows upwards. Slow growth. The blue leaves turn yellowish during fall.

Sempervivum (Houseleek)

The beauty of a rosette composed of many leaves.

Country of origin: Europe
How to propagate: Root separation

The leaves are tightly stacked to form an exceptionally beautiful rosette. There are so many varieties and so many similar types that it is difficult to distinguish one variety from another. After flowering, the plant will die.

| 1 | 2 | 3 | **4** | **5** | **6** | **7** | 8 | 9 | 10 | 11 | 12 |

※ **When the flower blooms, the stem withers.**

Growing Tip

It is very cold-hardy and can be grown outdoors at any time. This plant is easier to grow outdoors, as it should be grown in full sun. It's best not to grow it in a greenhouse. It is characterized by its ability to grow as a runner and to grow in clusters. When you want to increase the number of plants, divide them.

'Ashes of roses'
Overall purple color. Leaf surface is covered with hairs and the leaves form a large rosette.

'Rita Jane'
Green rosette with a purple center.

Calcarae
Only the leaf tips are purple. The leaves form large rosettes.

Arachnoideum
Leaf tips covered with hairs. In winter, it is especially hairy and the rosette is tight.

Senecio (Ragworts)

A cool silver-green family.

Country of origin: South Africa
How to propagate: Beheading

The sap has a distinctive fragrance. The leaves and stems are covered with white powder. Many varieties have interesting patterns on the veins of the leaves and stems. The flowers are unique and bloom well. It does not flower well if sunlight is insufficient.

| 1 | 2 | 3 | 4 | 5 | 6 | 7 | 8 | 9 | 10 | 11 | 12 |

Growing Tip

Since they grow in the cool season, replanting and propagation should be done in the fall. The root system, especially for the woody varieties, does not grow in summer. The vine varieties such as the *peregrinus* will grow in a slightly shaded area in summer. They will do well if they are watered throughout the year, but water more sparingly in mid-summer.

Rowleyanus (a.k.a String of Pearls)
Grows on a vine with green bell-like round leaves. Give a little water even in midsummer.

Kleiniiformis
Only the tips of the leaves spread out. It is a woody species and grows upwards as the lower leaves wither.

Serpens (a.k.a Blue Chalksticks)
The veins of the leaves stand out clearly and turn red during foliage season. It grows slowly.

Antandroi
Leaves are sharp and grow upward. Fast growing.

Articulatus
The stem grows large and produces leaves only at the top. Leaves drop off during the dormant season.

Citriformis
Leaves are a unique teardrop shape. A long-stemmed species with leaves only on the upper part of the stem.

Stapelia

Huernia

Grotesque flowers are beautiful too.

Country of origin: South Africa
How to propagate: Beheading

The genus is characterized by its spiny shoots and unusual, rather smelly flowers (designed to attract pollinators). Nicknamed the Lifesaver Cactus (though it is not a cactus) for the ring some species have around the center of their blooms. Flowers grow only on newly-sprouted branches, so a plant that produces shoot after shoot is ideal.

Growing Tip

Since it is sensitive to cold, leave it to rest and refrain from watering in winter. You can use branch cuttings for propagation. The divided plants should be left unplanted to dry out until spring. They may look quite shriveled—don't let that worry you. They will be fine to plant in spring.

1 2 3 4 5 6 7 8 9 10 11 12
※ **Flowering period may vary slightly depending on the variety.**

The Cacti

Eminent among succulents is the cactus family. Because there are so many different species, the term "cactus" has taken on a life of its own, but cacti are succulents too. They are in fact the most unique and evolved form of succulent. Their ability to survive, adapt and evolve has made them a powerful life force, Please take some time to know and enjoy these vibrant plants.

Astrophytum
Asterias (Sand-dollar cactus)

Flat, rounded shape in neatly divided segments called ribs. Each rib has the same beautiful speckled pattern. The round spots are the flower areoles that have bloomed and are moving downward as the plant grows. The flowers are yellow, large, and bloom in the center.

Mammillaria
Voburnensis

The spikes are very short and black, contrasting beautifully with the yellow spikes on the flower seat. Many yellow hairs appear on the flower areoles, from which several small white flowers bloom in a ray pattern. The young come out sideways and grow in clusters, growing slowly.

Echinocactus
Horizonthalonius
(Devil's head cactus)

Pale, white powdery skin. The spines growing from its areoles are a reddish color that becomes especially vivid during the growing season. Flowers are large and pink. This is a large-sphered cactus, slow-growing but relatively easy.

Lophophora
Diffusa (False Peyote)

This is a charming cactus with tufts of hair emerging from the flower areoles. The body is spherical but a little flatter and broader than many other round cacti and its ribs are not precisely defined. The flowers are small, and small flowers are produced from the hairs in the center. *Diffusa* grows faster and becomes a larger sphere than the typical *Casuarinas* of the same genus.

Epithelantha
Micromeris

A charming ovoid cactus that can grow singly or in clumps, as shown here. It is characterized by the spines that cover its body, very fine and worth observing through a magnifying glass. It has a concave center that sprouts lovely flowers.

Gymnocalycium
Denudatum

These deep green, slightly flattened spheres are covered with golden spines that grow in various, often spidery shapes and become brighter in color during the growing season. The skin is a shiny, solid green. Flowers grow from the top and can actually exceed the sphere's size.

Rhipsalis
Cereuscula

This genus is characterized by its cascading form. Stems form clumps by connecting at their edges. It grows relatively quickly, and in warmer months it will sprout new plantlets. These plantlets grow thin and long and produce more offspring at their tips.

Mammillaria
Hahniana (Old lady cactus)

Characterized by the long, shiny, pure white hair that grows all over its body, which grows into a flattened sphere. It produces an array of deep pink flowers that, on some of the many species in this genus, form a crown.

This plant is unique in the way it grows in a series of flat, round leaves. All plants in this genus grow in this way. It produces many young sprouts during its growth period. It can be easily propagated by beheading.

Opuntia
Prickly Pear

This is a columnar, upward-growing cactus characterized by beautiful red spines on its top. The lower part is covered with amazing long hair. It will not flower until it is quite large.

Espostoa
Mirabilis

A beautiful variety with long, flat spines protruding from the green sphere. If you look closely at the body, you'll see that its surface is pleated. This form evolved to increase the area for photosynthesis and reduce the area exposed to the sun to deter moisture loss. It produces large white flowers with purple streaks in the center.

Stenocactus
Lloydii

This cactus looks hard and solid, like a white rock. The surface is covered with spots and has white, rough, matte texture. It grows slowly and should be cared for patiently. When it reaches a certain spherical shape, it'll start growing upward. It produces a large yellow flower in the center at the top.

Astrophytum
Myriostigma

This is a pillar cactus, so it grows upward. Its form is rather like a dripping candle. The surface is covered with a fine white powder that gives the plant a blue-gray cast. There are short spines at the end of the cob. Flowers do not bloom until the plant is quite large.

Myrtillocactus
Geometrizans
(Blue Myrtle Cactus)

The dense white spines have earned this plant the nickname Snowball. It usually grows as a single sphere, but this photo shows a clustered type with many offspring. The flowers are pink with streaks and bloom in a ray pattern. The flowers are relatively large for this genus. It likes regular watering in summer.

Mammillaria
Candida

Coiled spines (painless to the touch) cover the surface. Young spines range from red to purple, fading to more of a pink or blush as they age. It is a slow grower, but if you water it well during the growing season, it will thrive and grow large. It produces very large, beautiful pink flowers.

Echinocereus
Pectinatus var.rigidissimus

The oval-shaped, short, white spines grow in a uniform pattern on the surface. The plant starts out spherical, but becomes cylindrical as grows. The large flowers vary from white to purplish to stripy combinations of the two. It does not tolerate humidity in summer, so it should be kept in a well-ventilated area.

Turbinicarpus
Valdezianus

Mammillaria
Plumosa (Feather Cactus)

Appears as a series of white, fluffy spheres that give off a sense of mystery. When the spheres grow to a certain size, they produce offspring, which in turn produce, and so on, creating a sort of bubbling effect. The spines are curly and painless to touch. Flowers scatter across the globes in winter.

Stenocactus
Albatus

This beautiful variety has a spherical body covered with a series of long and short cream or white spines. Purple flowers bloom in the center in early spring.

Gymnocalycium
Friedrichii variegata

A beautiful variety with vivid red and/or yellow and green coloring. Spines form at the tips of ridges along the ribs. It likes water, and if grown in humid conditions, it will have a fresh, reptilian-like skin.

Mammillaria
Dioica
(Strawberry Cactus)

When this species grows into an oval shape, it produces offspring and begins to grow in clusters. It is covered with short white spines and hairs.. Small deep pink flowers bloom from the white spines. It is relatively easy to grow,

Grouping Succulents and Cacti

Once you have successfully cultivated individual succulents and cacti, one of the most enjoyable aspects is to have fun decorating them by matching their colors and shapes. In this theme, we introduce succulents and cacti that are pleasing to the eye. Collect your favorite succulents and enjoy them as interior decorations.

Enjoy beautiful flower-like leaf formations
Echeveria and *Sedeveria* have leaves that spread out like flowers. Many new hybrids have come out in recent years. Groupings of this genus can easily resemble a flower garden.

Setosa

'Pink Ruby'

'Topsy Turvy'

Lilacina

Pulidonis

'Black Prince'

'Albert Baynes'

'Douglas Huth'

'Momotaro'

'Green Emerald'

Leaf color changes with the seasons
The plump leaves come in a variety of
shapes and colors, and even change color
as the leaves turn red. The leaves do not
decolorize, but gradually fade to a lighter
shade as the weather gets warmer. It has
a somewhat human charm when it grows
fatter and firmer during the foliage season.

Awayuki

Titubans

Agvoides

Moranii

'Pink Pretty'

Group plants by unifying colors
One of the charms of succulents is that there are so many varieties, but with so many to choose from, deciding how to group and display them can be overwhelming. When it doubt, use color to decide what to combine. By going for unity of color, the shapes and patterns of the leaves will stand out more, and the display will look tidier.

Frizzle Sizzle

Cylindrica

Kaimagyoku

Two Story Pagoda

Eve's Pin Cactus

Shizukuishi

The pleasure of arranging and decorating

Some types will just keep growing upward and branch out in all directions. Seeing a variety of shapes and sizes lined up on a windowsill is especially nice. Like a bonsai, if you grow your succulent in a small pot for a long time, even a plant like the *Arboreum* will have small leaves and a miniature appearance.

Arboreum   Mikaeri-Bijin   Affinis   'Perle Von Nurnberg'   Paraguayense

Soft greens and bright yellows

Succulents are not monochromatic in color; many of them have a gradation. The gradation makes the shape more three-dimensional and beautiful. By arranging several single pots side by side, you can enjoy an aesthetic similar to a group planting. You can also use a book or similar as a riser, or change the arrangement according to your mood.

Oncoclada

Happy Bean

'Golden Girl'

Cereuscula

Elongata

Opuntia

Sunrise Mum

Cacti collection

Ah—the beauty of cacti forms! Even small-size cacti can flaunt beautiful shapes and colors. If you collect cacti in matching pots, you can bring out their characteristics even more. Really observe the color and shape of the spines. Try holding them in the palm of your hand and viewing them through a magnifying glass.

Myriostigma

Indian Corn Cob

Ashura

Pseudopulcherrima

Leninghausii

Graciliis

Arizona Snowcap

Glaucescens

Latispinus

Planting Haworthia

There are so many species in this genus that it's fun to make groupings consisting just of *Haworthia*. If you plant them in a large pot like this, you can enjoy them as if they're in their natural habitat. Plants that clump together like rocks—you can enjoy watching your arrangement grow.

Mysterious white plant

The *Dudleya* genus is said to be the whitest of the succulents. The white powder gives the plants an otherworldly, mysterious look. There aren't many other white plants like this one. If you expose it to light, the whiteness will increase, so don't forget to let it bathe in the sun by the window or on the porch or balcony.

Monkey Tree

Brittonii

Millotii

Cotyledon orbiculata
'Fuku Daruma'

'Fanfare'

Parodia

Things to Keep in Mind When Growing Cacti

Many people have the impression that cacti do not need water, so they do not water even small cacti. The body of a cactus is like a tank that stores water. And as smaller tanks store less, a small cactus needs water in order to grow. If you take just a little time to learn about how to care for cacti, they grow slowly, but you'll have the cute little guy with you for a long time.

Watering

It is said that more than 95% of a cactus's body is water. The larger the cactus, the more water it can store, so it needs to be watered less frequently.

Some cacti can live for a year without watering, absorbing moisture from the air and storing it in their bodies without withering. However, cacti with small bodies need to be watered from time to time because they can only store a small amount of water. They will not die without water, but if you want them to grow nicely, they need water from time to time. When watering, give enough to soak the soil—water should be coming through the pot's drainage hole. If the pot doesn't have a drainage hole, water the plant enough to moisten the soil completely. If the plant is getting dehydrated its body will wrinkle, which is a sign that it needs to be watered.

Placement

Spines evolved for shading purposes, covering the body and providing it with cooling protection against intense sun. To keep the spines beautiful, keep them in a well-sunlit place. On the other hand, if the spines are short and the sphere is exposed, it is best to keep the plants slightly shaded from sun in midsummer. Be careful not to suddenly expose plants that have been living in low light to bright sunlight, as this may cause burn-like scars. Keeping cacti in a sunny location throughout the year is ideal--again, modifying sun exposure in accordance with the plant's natural shading.

Fertilization

Because of its slow growth, add a small amount of a long-acting (slow-release) fertilizer when planting or replanting. A strong, fast-acting fertilizer is not recommended, as fertilizer burn may occur.

How to grow more

Grow from seed. Various types can be produced from seeds, and they are very hardy. Pillar cacti can also be propagated by beheading.

Cactus flowers

We often hear it said that "If you love them, they will bloom," which isn't entirely true. During the growing season, give your cactus plenty of sun and love, and during the dormant season, cut off water and grow it meticulously. This is the trick to growing cacti well and to making them bloom beautifully. Specifically, during the growing season, expose it to the sun as much as possible. The dormant period for most cacti will be in winter, so watering should be reduced during this season. In desert-like areas, cacti rest during periods of no rainfall, and then replenish water and grow all at once during the rainy months. It is also a good idea to repot the plants about once a year. This is all you need to do to keep your cactus blooming beautifully.

> Yukio Mukaiyama talks about the history of succulents in his country, and offers tips on how to grow them.
>
> Misa Matsuyama is a great admirer of Yukio Mukaiyama and looks upon him as a teacher. She interviewed him at Futawa Garden, a nursery he runs in Sakura City, Chiba Prefecture. On the day of the interview, store traffic was hopping even though it was a weekday afternoon. We asked Mr. Mukaiyama, a succulents specialist, what succulents are and his tips on how to grow them beautifully.

Succulents have a very long history

Q **How would you describe a succulent in a nutshell?**

A We now tend to distinguish succulents from cacti, but originally cacti were also classified as succulents. Both are fleshy and carry water. In fact, the majority of succulents are in the cactus family. Cacti are from the Cactaceae family, while succulents come from a multitude of families. Most of the commonly-grown succulents come from the Crassulaceae family, from which we get Echeveria, Sedum, Crassula, Kalanchoe, and more; and the Euphorbiaceae family, from which we get Euphorbia species. Most of these come from Africa and Mexico and like cacti, they're accustomed to harsh desert conditions. Have you ever heard of the CAM plant? The "C" in CAM is for Crassulaceae, and the "A" is for acid. M is for metabolism.

Q **That's photosynthesis in reverse, right?**

A Yes, yes. Because they grow in dry areas during the day, they try to photosynthesize like non-succulent plants, but if their pores are open, they get too dry. So they close their stomata during the day so they don't breathe carbon dioxide. Then, when the temperature drops at night and the body water does not evaporate, they open their pores to absorb carbon dioxide and return it to the body in the form of organic acids (carboxylic acids). During the daytime, when the sun is shining, the body stores the carbon dioxide gas, which is then used to carry out photosynthesis. Such plants are called CAM plants. Most succulents are like that. And then there are the cattleyas. And cattleyas are succulents, too.

Q **I see. Where did you study succulents?**

A I didn't really study them, but I've been doing this for 50 years. After 50 years, it's natural to me.

Q **But you didn't know anything about them when you started working with plants, right? You didn't consult books or anything like that?**

A I didn't read any books. If I had to say where I first learned about succulents, I credit my middle and high school science textbooks. Those books are the best reference. When people ask me if we carry any good books on growing cacti and succulents, I say "Read your junior high school science textbooks."

Q **(Laughs) Fifty years ago, I don't think the word "succulent" was even known to the general public.**

A I disagree. I think everyone was somewhat aware of them. As for when they became popular, right after the war, Disney made a nature documentary called *The Living Desert*. That film helped make cacti very popular.

Q **Did you like it when you saw it, Mukaiyama-san?**

A I've been interested in plants since I was in elementary school, and I bought my first cactus at a festival. That was before the war. People seem to have the mistaken impression that this hobby of growing succulent plants is something new, but there was a magazine published in the early Showa period by the Japan Rose Society. They ran an article about a cacti exhibition held at Ginza Mitsukoshi, and from what the photos showed, there were definitely things on display that were as good as anything we see now. So the interest in succulents is pretty old.

Q **The names of succulents are difficult to find, and in Japan, the use of Kanji characters gives a sense of the times, but did you start out by importing them?**

A Yes, yes. Before the war, most of them were imported from Germany. Germany was even in contact with us during the war. So, during the Meiji period (1868–1912), more and more products were imported from Germany.

Q **So the Meiji Era was the first?**

A It goes back earlier than that. Maybe since the Edo period. Are you familiar with Shokusanjin (Oota Nanpo)? There seems to be a reference in some of his work to what we now call Euphorbia, and it indicates that succulent plants have been in Japan since the Edo period.

Q **So when did they become popular in general?**

A They were quite popular even before the war. There was a cactus garden in Nagoya called Kozoen, which specialized in cacti, and they published a magazine called *Shaboteno-Kenkyu*. That was before the war. There was also a cactus garden called Kyorakuen in Fujisawa City, Kanagawa Prefecture, which was established in the Meiji Era.

Q In the past, were succulents and cacti raised among the nobility?

A That's right. In the past, these plants were rare, and their prices were so high that the general public couldn't afford them.

Q So it was a really high-end product.

A I heard that the more expensive varieties were bought on a monthly installment basis. I didn't have the money to buy them myself, so I bought cheap ones that were sold at fairs and grew them. Well, we could go on and on—there is no end to the history of succulents and cacti (laughs).

The trick is "More light!"

Q What do you think about the recent popularity of succulents?

A I'm happy as long as everything sells because, after all, we're running a business (laugh). It seems that Korea and China are importing a lot, and that has created a worldwide boom.

Q What do you think about the future of the succulent world?

A I said that *Haworthia* is popular now, but I don't mean to imply it will go out of fashion in the future. Everyone says that the genus will be developed through selective breeding and that plants will increase in number and become cheaper. The reason for this is that you can enjoy these plants indoors. For example, cacti can't grow without sunlight but *Haworthia* can be grown

in semi-shade, and if you use both fluorescent lamps and LEDs, you can grow them even in places with poor sunlight. It's already popular as an indoor plant. It doesn't take up much space. In that sense, I don't think *Haworthia* will go out of fashion. Echeveria is also easy to grow and collect, but Echeveria doesn't show beautiful colors without strong light. If you are growing for the first time, I think *Haworthia* is an easy and satisfying choice.

Q What made you start growing succulents??

A I became friends with an Indonesian who had come to Japan to buy cacti, so I went to Indonesia to visit. I stayed there for about a month, and during that time, I heard that Australia has a lot of interesting things to see and do. So we thought "let's go together!" We went to Australia, and I discovered that succulents grow naturally there. Because of the arid soil, ordinary plants will die. That's why they plant Echeverias there, just like we plant pansies and violas in Japan. It's dry and the sun is strong, so they grow beautifully. I was like, "Wow, that's beautiful!" I bought some echeveria over there and got hooked on it.

Q These are Mukaiyama-san's treasures that you are about to introduce. Is there a reason why you chose these among many?

A I put out the best *Haworthia* products that are popular right now. Small plants are difficult to grow. It's almost impossible for inexperienced gardeners to raise them. And Echeveria is so beautiful to look at. Also, what we import from Africa cannot be cultivated in Japan.

Q Finally, do you have any advice for first-time succulent growers?

A In general, succulents are drought tolerant, so just keep that in mind. Don't water excessively. Don't keep them in a place that's too humid. But because they are plants, they still need watering. As long as you can balance that, there is nothing to worry about. And the fleshy ones are storing a lot of water, which can freeze. If the temperature drops even a little below 32°F/ 0°C, your plant may freeze. You know how they say not to water in winter? That is to make the plant supple and hard to freeze. It takes two to three months to make them shrivel up. If you want to drain water, you should start in the fall.

Q The seedlings in your store are very unique, with beautiful colors and very tidy shapes.

A That's just because I'm lazy and don't water them (laughs). I don't fertilize them or replant them (laughs). Well, I'd like to, but I can't get it done in time. That's why they shrivel up. Maybe it's because their nursery environment is similar to the local environment. Maybe that's why their color is darker and richer. If a succulent gets a lot of sunlight and little water, it will naturally become hard. The harder you make it, the stronger the plant will be. If you have good sunlight, you can grow them hard. If you keep them in the shade, they will all become brittle. If you grow them in a room with "normal" watering, it's natural that they will become sprouts (laughs). That's why they tend to rot. This is important. If you keep the minimum temperature at 50°F/10°C and the maximum at 77°F/25°C, you will have strong and beautiful succulents. If your succulents only get half daylight, you can strengthen them by using reflective light such as reflective paper on the back, or by adding fluorescent or LED lights. Growing succulents is indeed easy. They will grow for two to three years if you just leave them there. But then they are only alive. To make them truly vivid, you only need to do what I just mentioned. The secret is "more light!" The trick is "more light!" Easy, isn't it?

Yukio Mukaiyama

Futawa Garden
258 Kamishizuhara, Sakura City, Chiba Prefecture
http://www.kk.iij4u.
or.jp/~yukicact/

The pride of Futawa Garden
The world of succulents

Mukaiyama talked a lot about succulents on the previous pages. At Futawa, a wide variety of succulents can be found. Here and elsewhere in the world some of the rarest and costliest succulents can run several hundred dollars for a single plant.

These are plants that can range from $5 to $100 or more depending on the species and the specimen. Actually seeing the plant's condition before buying is optimal. If buying plants online, choose vendors that provide good information and carefully check their reviews. Research the best season for buying a plant that requires shipment, and consider the region of both source and destination.

Maughanii (Dragon)

Maughanii

Milky Way

Retsusa

Haworthia Comptoniana

Haworthia Retusa f. Geraldii

Truncata

Aristata

Right: Party Dress *Left*: Strawberry Hearts

Right: Shoki *Left*: Banbutsusou

Right: Mexican Giant *Left*: Brittonii

Succulent Arrangements

Because succulents are hardy, there are many ways to enjoy them. You can give them as gifts, wear them and decorate your space with them. Another charm of succulents is that they can be planted in containers other than standard pots.

An arrangement of cut flowers

1 **Tools/materials:** Floral foam, container, floral tape, scissors, wire, cut succulent plantlets (we used Alice Evans, Moon Beauty, Sedum rubrotinctum, Sedum pachyphyllum, Burrito, Sermentosa) stems of Eucalyptus, Lavender, Epidendrum). You'll also need a sheet of plastic wrap.

2 Moisten the floral foam and cut it into the shape of the container. Layer the container with the plastic wrap at the bottom and insert it with the floral foam.

3 Cut the leftover plastic wrap, consider the placement you'd like, then add the wired flowers as described on pages 101, steps 2–6.

4 Succulents may wither and die due to high water content when placed too deeply in the floral foam, so let them "float" a little.

5 To avoid showing the base, cover the base with leaves.

Finished

Using Succulents in a Floral Arrangement

Succulents are becoming increasingly popular as a floral material, as seen in cut flower arrangements these days. The trick to making them last longer is to keep them out of water. Unlike other plants, succulents have a tendency to root when they dry out, so when arranging. For example, if you wire them and let the cut ends float a little instead of placing them directly on the floral foam. This way they can rejuvenate without rotting. When other flowers are dying, it is always the succulents that remain at the end. Only succulents can be planted in the soil and enjoyed after enjoying the flowers.

Use an egg carton as a planter

1 Tools/materials: Succulent plantlets (We used Sedum rubrotinctum, Golden Ball Cactus, Prickly Pear, Cornephylium Elongata, Notocactus, Saguro Cactus, Tsukubane, 'Margarette Reppin'), Sphagnum moss, egg carton.

2 Moisten the moss all over.

3 Wrap the root of each plant with a moss ball.

4 After wrapping the root ball, plant it in the egg carton.

5 Determine the placement by looking at the overall balance.

\ **Finished** /

Planting with Sphagnum Moss

When arranging with Sphagnum moss, firmly squeeze it out to some extent at the time of planting to remove excess water. Be careful where you place it because if it is placed in a poorly ventilated area, mold will grow before the roots emerge. If you use a large amount of moss, it will not dry properly and the roots will easily rot. Sphagnum moss is also suitable for use in small pots that are difficult to fill with soil. If you want to use it in a large pot, keep to only the top 1–2 inches (3–5 cm) of the pot, using regular blended soil for the lower part of the pot.

1 **Tools/materials:** Preserved Hydrangea, floral tape, wire, cut succulents (Clavatum, Ghost plant, Burrito).

2 Remove the lower leaves of the succulents for easier wiring.

3 With the wire, pierce the plant at the base and fold the wire down, forming something of a U shape.

4 Wrap the wired stem of the succulent with floral tape, starting at the base of the succulent, as shown.

5 This is how it should look after you finish wrapping it.

6 Wire the hydrangea by making the U between the center two branches. Wrap as in steps 4–5.

7 Here we have all the plants wrapped in floral tape.

8 Combine while observing the balance, and when you've settled on an overall shape, tape all the pieces together. After wrapping, adjust the entire piece.

Finished

1 **Tools/materials:**
Sisal hemp, preserved hydrangea, cut succulent seedlings (Titubans, shuurei, Paraguayense, Adolphi, Treleasei, Kalanchoe crenata), wire, ribbon, floral tape, nippers, scissors.

2 Separate hydrangeas by clusters.

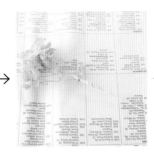

3 Wire and wrap floral tape as described in steps 2–6 on page 101.

4 Succulents should be wired easily by removing the lower leaves.

5 Do the same with the other succulents and wire all the floral materials.

6 Balance and adjust the shape to your liking, and if there is a gap between plants, fill it with sisal hemp.

7 After balancing the whole arrangement, secure it with tape.

8 Finally, hide the back side with sisal hemp so that it cannot be seen.

9 Adjust so that the overall shape is rounded.

10 Wrap the ribbon around the handle.

11 Tie tightly at the base then tie a bow with another length of ribbon.

Finished

1 **Tools/materials:** Haworthia, beaker, fertilizer, akadama soil (medium grain), ornamental stones, soil, tweezers, soil scoop.

2 Remove plantlets from plastic pots. First loosen by squeezing the pot...

3 ...then pull gently to release the plant.

4 Remove lower leaves with tweezers.

5 Remove old roots.

6 Old roots have been removed.

7 Fill the beaker with enough akadama soil to fill the bottom.

8 Add enough soil to cover the akadama soil.

9 Add fertilizer.

10 Check the plantlet-to-beaker height ratio.

11 Once the height is determined, add soil to create a little peak in the middle to allow the roots to spread easily.

12 Center the plantlet over the peak.

13 Add soil toward the edges to prevent soil from getting between the leaves.

14 Tap the soil lightly while holding the plant.

15 Decorate with ornamental stones.

16 Finished!

Plant mini cacti in terracotta

1 **Tools/materials:** Mini cacti, fertilizer, newspaper, potting net, terracotta pot, tweezers, soil, soil scoop.

2 Put the cut newspaper in the bottom hole of the pot.

3 Place the bottom netting on top of the newspaper.

4 Put in the plantlets to be planted, adjust the height as you add in soil.

5 Fill the pot to the desired height.

6 Add fertilizer.

7 After adding fertilizer, add soil again.

8 Decide on the placement of the mini cacti.

9 Once the location is determined, plant the mini cacti one by one. At this point, use tweezers to dig into the soil and push the plantlet into the soil.

10 Fill the area around the plantlet with soil to secure them in place.

TIP

You can plant all three at the same time! You can also hold them together then put them in while holding them down!

11 Plant the second and third cactus in the same manner.

12 After all the plantlets have been planted, add soil around them again to hold them in place.

13 While holding down the plants, lightly tap the planter to level the soil.

14 Finished!

Create a large grouping

1 **Tools to be used:** Pots, seedlings, medium Akadama soil, fertilizer, soil, soil scoop, tweezers.

2 Fill the pot with enough akadama soil to cover the bottom of the pot.

3 Add enough soil to cover akadama soil layer.

4 Add fertilizer.

5 Decide where to position each plant.

6 When removing the plant from the pot, insert the tweezers gently and pull it out.

7 Use a cloth to handle the cactus so you won't be pricked. Remove soil by loosening the rootball.

8 Similarly, clean up the roots of the other plants.

9 Plant the main cactus. If it hurts to touch with bare hands, use gardening gloves or a cloth.

10·11 Plant the other plantlets in order, starting with the cactus.

12 For relatively small plantlets, grasp with tweezers along the stem and insert them. Fill in the gaps between the larger plantlets.

13 Here is the grouping with all the plantlets in place. Taller ones are planted in the back for balance, which helps accentuate the plants in front.

14 Finally, fill in the gaps with soil.

15 For large plants, use tweezers to push the soil deeper into the pot, or tap the pot to level the soil.

16 Finished!

Plant Echeveria in a mug

1 **Tools/materials:** Mug, Echeveria, soil, soil scoop, tweezers.

2 Remove the seedling from the plastic pot.

3 Remove the lower leaves with tweezers.

4 Slightly loosen the roots and remove overgrown roots.

5 Fill the cup with soil.

6 Place the seedling in the cup, adjust its position, fix it in place, and fill in the gaps with soil.

7 Turn the pot to fill the entire area with soil.

8 Tap the soil lightly while holding the plant, and you're done.

INDEX OF PLANTS

"Books to Span the East and West"

Tuttle Publishing was founded in 1832 in the small New England town of Rutland, Vermont (USA). Our core values remain as strong today as they were then—to publish best-in-class books which bring people together one page at a time. In 1948, we established a publishing outpost in Japan—and Tuttle is now a leader in publishing English-language books about the arts, languages and cultures of Asia. The world has become a much smaller place today and Asia's economic and cultural influence has grown. Yet the need for meaningful dialogue and information about this diverse region has never been greater. Over the past seven decades, Tuttle has published thousands of books on subjects ranging from martial arts and paper crafts to language learning and literature—and our talented authors, illustrators, designers and photographers have won many prestigious awards. We welcome you to explore the wealth of information available on Asia at www.tuttlepublishing.com.

Published by Tuttle Publishing, an imprint of Periplus Editions (HK) Ltd.

www.tuttlepublishing.com

ISBN 978-0-8048-5597-6

ZOHO KAITEIBAN sol X sol NO TANIKUSHOKUBUTSU, SABOTEN WO SODATEYO (Boutique Mook no. 1503)
Copyright © 2020 Boutique-sha, Inc.
English Translation rights arranged with Boutique-sha, Inc. through Japan UNI Agency, Inc. Tokyo

English Translation © 2023 by Periplus Editions (HK) Ltd.
Translated from Japanese by HL Language Services

Original Japanese edition
Author Misa Matsuyama (sol x sol)
Interviewer Yukio Mukaiyama (Niwaen)
Photography Mari Harada
Book design and Illustrations Shuko Miura
Editors Ryohei Maruyama, Chizuru Tomiya
Publisher Akira Naito

Distributed by:

North America, Latin America & Europe
Tuttle Publishing
364 Innovation Drive
North Clarendon
VT 05759-9436 U.S.A.
Tel: (802) 773-8930 Fax: (802) 773-6993
info@tuttlepublishing.com
www.tuttlepublishing.com

Asia Pacific
Berkeley Books Pte. Ltd.
3 Kallang Sector, #04-01
Singapore 349278
Tel: (65) 6741-2178 Fax: (65) 6741-2179
inquiries@periplus.com.sg
www.tuttlepublishing.com

27 26 25 24 23   10 9 8 7 6 5 4 3 2 1
Printed in China   2306EP

TUTTLE PUBLISHING® is the registered trademark of Tuttle Publishing, a division of Periplus Editions (HK) Ltd.